Park

Mazinaigan Waakaaigan
P.O. Box 529
Bayfield, WI. 54814

LOGGERHEAD TURTLE

LOGGERHEAD TURTLE

Survivor from the Sea

words by JACK DENTON SCOTT

photographs by OZZIE SWEET

G. P. Putnam's Sons · New York

Text copyright © 1974 by Jack Denton Scott
Photographs copyright © 1974 by Ozzie Sweet
All rights reserved. Published simultaneously in
Canada by Longman Canada Limited, Toronto.
Library of Congress Catalog Card Number: 73-83993
SBN: GB-399-60869-9
SBN: TR-399-20379-6
PRINTED IN THE UNITED STATES OF AMERICA
Designed by Bobye List
All Ages
Second Impression

$\mathcal{E}$VEN though it is just before dusk, if you were sitting in a boat on the window-clear waters of the Atlantic Ocean off the Florida coast, you would be able to see straight down for 50 feet. Beyond that distance the bottom of the sea is a bluish haze. A sort of patchy carpet of undersea growth shows through, and there is an occasional gleam of sand.

Looking harder, you can see green moss and pink coral. Swarming around the coral are brightly banded coral fish and sun-yellow grunts. Occasionally a blue parrot fish darts past, and fat black angelfish with white mouths lie like pieces of mosaic. A school of mullet passes in a flash of silver. Lacy purple sea fans wave gently in the underwater current. Sea anemones, looking like blossoming iris beds of blues, greens, and reds, wait for tiny fish to swim into their petallike poisonous tentacles.

But there is no predatory action now; the underwater world is peaceful. Like the impending dusk, it appears to be waiting. Suddenly, from the depths of 132 feet, a large black shadow begins to rise, bursting into the shallower waters, scattering the fish, and passing like a boat through the deadly garden of sea anemones.

As the shadow shoots toward the surface, even though the water is changing color, what you can now see is a huge, fearsome creature, riding the tide as easily as a bird flies—its large, flipperlike limbs cleaving the water cleanly as oars.

The familiar four-inch garden turtle is suddenly blown into 300 pounds, measuring 4 feet across the back, its scaly skull massive, horny bill protruding, reddish-brown oval back shell breaking the water—an antediluvian monster risen from the deep. Head moving in a side-to-side snake motion, it is partially out of the water now and seems to be coasting in on slippery slides of the sea. It glides by, water churning around it, and never notices your boat. It has poor eyesight, and it is on a mission that is occupying its full attention, one of the most important of its life. A miracle of survival brought this armored reptile here this spring evening to lay its eggs.

Two hundred million years ago, long before that violent age of giants when the dinosaurs tried to destroy the world and succeeded only in destroying themselves, there were twenty-four genera of turtles. Today there are eleven. These eleven, including this one appearing in the ocean off Florida, have remained largely unchanged for 150,000,000 years.

They survived even when the seemingly indestructible 50-ton *Brachiosaurus* gasped its last breath, probably because of their unusual protective turtle structure. So perfect is that structure that turtles have made fewer physical compromises to evolution than other creatures and are difficult to harm. One scientist called them tanks that can swim and survive underwater. Their top shell is called a carapace and is made up of grown-over widened ribs; underneath is the whitish plastron. Both sections are covered with tough, horny plates, and their legs are attached within their ribs. Skulls are large and horny-hard, beaks are strong and sharp, and although turtles are toothless, they can eat plant and animal food, everything from insects to shellfish and fish.

Because they are reptiles, turtles, especially sea turtles, have a very low metabolic rate and do not require much oxygen. According to the size of the turtle, they need three to four hundred times less oxygen than a man does; thus, they can stay below the water for long periods without surfacing for air. By a complicated breathing system, using the pharynx (that section of the digestive tract that extends from the nasal cavities to the larynx) as a fish uses a gill—taking in and discharging water to obtain oxygen—one turtle lived completely underwater for eight days, according to a researcher. There is also the remarkable achievement of one turtle living for twenty-four hours in a chamber of pure nitrogen.

This most unusual ancient reptile is of the Chelonian order, which falls into two suborders, the Cryptodirea, which can hide and protect their heads by telescoping them into their shells, and the Pleurodirea, which lay their heads horizontally to the side.

This is *Caretta caretta*, the loggerhead turtle, of the suborder Cryptodirea, a head hider, a mysterious sea turtle which still has the scientists puzzled about many aspects of its existence.

It is one of five species of sea turtles in the world—the loggerheads, the ridleys, the hawksbills, the green turtles, and the leatherbacks.

The loggerhead is a restless wanderer of the seas. No one knows the full extent of its journeys. But it is known that the Atlantic loggerhead ranges the Atlantic Ocean and the Mediterranean Sea, from parts of South America to Canada, even near Scotland, also off the Canary Islands and the coast of West Africa. It likes coastal bays, but it is unpredictable and has been seen 500 miles out at sea and found in southern marshes, traveling up creeks or small streams. It has been reported that the loggerhead has even made long journeys up the Mississippi River. A hardy, adaptable turtle of amiable disposition that can handle itself under most conditions, it is not aggressive but, if attacked, can take care of itself. There is a case reported by a leading scientist of one loggerhead weighing more than 600 pounds that had escaped from a Connecticut fish dealer who for some reason had pierced holes through its paddlelike feet. Enraged, the turtle tore down the planked pen it was put in as if it were constructed of matchsticks and found its way to a harbor, not far from Norwalk, Connecticut. The fish dealer offered a $50 reward for its capture. Five expert fishermen went after it. They found the floating turtle asleep on the surface in the harbor, and one man speared it. The spear broke on the horny shell, and a one-hour battle was joined. The turtle tried to turn the boat over, while the five men beat it over the head with oars. The loggerhead broke all the oars and slashed the arm of one of the men. The turtle continued tipping the boat until it was nearly filled with water. Then it disappeared underwater, unharmed.

Loggerheads have also been observed calmly swimming among sharks. A loggerhead once attacked by a shark was seen by fishermen to raise itself out of the water and slap the surface loudly with its flippers, driving the shark away.

Fishermen have also seen it munching its way through a gang of deadly Portuguese men-of-war. It was thought that the poisonous sting from this large jellylike fish was deathly toxic to almost any living creature until the ever-surprising loggerhead was sighted actually lunching on the thing's stinging filaments. True, the turtle's head did appear to be slightly swollen, its eyes nearly shut, but other than that, no ill effects were reported.

When swimming, the loggerhead uses its fore flippers as gracefully as a bird in flight, and with the same up-and-down efficient stroke. It is among the fastest of the reptiles, its speed in the water sometimes comparable to that of a young man in top condition running as fast as he can. The loggerhead not only has control of its life on the water's surface, but is fast and agile underwater as well. This world that the sea turtle uses so effectively is larger than man's. It is so vast that no one has yet determined the variety and amount of life in the oceans. But scientists have proved that all life began in the sea (even ours), and that of all the living animals that are grouped in thirty-one classes, most members of all the major classes are in the sea.

Of them, as an advanced, modern reptile that has survived all the complex evolutionary multimillion-year changes, the sea turtle is one of the most important forms of life. And of the sea turtles, the loggerhead is among the most outstanding. The loggerhead prefers the continental shelf, which skirts the earth's coastlines where it slopes gradually away from shore to an area 500 feet deep. Because of the abundance of life there, this is the loggerhead's grocery story, its supermarket. In some places in the Atlantic, the home territory of the loggerhead, that shelf can reach out 100 miles. But off southeastern Florida, where many loggerheads are found, there isn't any continental shelf at all. A river in the ocean, called the Gulf Stream, moves so strongly and swiftly through that area that it vacuums the off-shore bottom clean, and there is no shelf-constructing undersea debris. Even so, there is much marine life to keep the loggerhead well fed.

Although technically classified as omnivorous, an eater of all foods, the loggerhead is mainly carnivorous, eating fish, crabs, oysters, conchs, jellyfish, sponges, and just about every kind of mollusk and crustacean. It has also been seen eating *Zostera*, marine grasses.

Despite its catholic appetite and its physical assets that make the sea its sanctuary and storehouse, it isn't just an easy grab-and-take world for the loggerhead. There are larger, fiercer creatures that will prey on the loggerhead if they can: killer whales, some kinds of sharks, and, the most dangerous—man, who hunts the sea turtles for their meat and eggs. Luckily for the loggerhead, however, most men prefer the green sea turtle. Its flesh is the main ingredient in turtle soups. But the loggerhead is eaten by some people, and its eggs are sought by man and other predators nearly everywhere.

The loggerhead, also something of a mountain climber, had a strenuous time getting to Florida's shores. Probably swimming 1,000 miles, it had many ups and downs because the largest mountain range in existence is part of this turtle's world. The Mid-Oceanic Ridge twists underwater between the continental landmasses for 40,000 miles through all the oceans. Lifting from 6,000 to 12,000 feet above the bottom of the seas, the peaks and pinnacles of this vast mountain ridge sometimes break through the surface of the water, forming islands like Ascension and the Azores.

Making their way over these sea mountains from great distances (perhaps from the mysterious, unknown regions where they sometimes disappear on migrations), the loggerheads normally seen swim at a somewhat leisurely rate of speed, lazily scissoring flippers, or sometimes just float on the sunlit sea, often sleeping on the surface.

Despite their size and not exactly handsome appearance, loggerheads have a magnetic personality, said by one expert who has studied them for years, to consist of "good-humored quaintness and elfin drollery." Another called them the pleasantly ugly, peacefully pugnacious English bulldogs of the sea. They have been observed romping on the water and playing with one another—ocean giants, cavorting like children at a seashore.

Jacques-Yves Cousteau, perhaps the world's leading expert on the sea and its creatures, says that sea turtles are models of patience and gentleness. Despite days he and his men spent diving among them, studying them, offering them food, moving them about, photographing them, he said that it seemed nearly impossible to make the turtles lose their tempers.

Mating takes place on the sea's surface just before nesting time. Yet it isn't this mating that fertilizes the eggs about to be laid but one that occurred many months before. It is believed that spermatozoa may stay in the reproductive region of the female after one mating and continue to fertilize for four years, with the female laying eggs as often as four times a year! This unusual storage system is probably another reason for the loggerhead's historical longevity, eliminating the necessity for frequent matings to ensure survival of the species. Thus, though turtles may actually mate at every spring nesting season, it really isn't necessary. The turtle earlier observed from the boat undoubtedly had coupled with a male (slightly smaller than the female, but with a much longer tail) not far from the Florida coast where it appeared.

If disturbed during mating, the female, usually the more aggressive, becomes timid and flees. The male refuses to be deterred and is actually dragged, still in the mating tie, through the water by the female until she is calm and active mating is resumed.

After mating, loggerheads seek the sandy beaches of the southern coast of the United States as favorite nurseries. Here two turtle spectaculars occur many times every spring.

If you had come to shore in your boat when you first saw the great loggerhead appear and determinedly head beachward, you would have witnessed one of the most dramatic and perilous pilgrimages in the animal world.

These great sea turtles spend all their lives in the sea, except during breeding season, usually from April through August. Then only the female leaves her watery world and comes to alien and hostile land to lay her eggs and precariously reproduce her own kind.

Pulled by a mysterious and fascinating reproductive instinct that science has yet to explain fully, the turtle temporarily returns to land, which its ancestors had forsaken as dangerous and uninhabitable 100,000,000 years ago.

(Scientists believe that there was a great dry spell in Cenozoic times, when many marine animals had to seek a new way of life on dry land. Some successfully made the change; some did not. Turtles were able to live in or out of water but made fewer concessions to the new way of life than most other animals, having proved through eons how superior they were in the seas. Thus, turtles did not completely adapt to land as other creatures were forced to, and when the world returned to normal and the drought passed, they went back to the marine existence to which they were so perfectly adjusted. Turtles could take land or leave it; mostly they left it. On land they were vulnerable, they were slow, and the sun made them uncomfortable; in water they were swift as a fish and physically secure in its depth or on its surface.)

Approaching land, the turtle suddenly slackens its speed, stopping the action of its flippers almost completely, letting the spring flood tide float it in. Its brown back glistens like polished wood as it arches above the water. A full moon, which often accompanies the latter half of the flood tide, is rising, flooding the beach with clear light.

The sea breaks on the shore, then creams and foams around the turtle as she stands in the surf. Seemingly aware that she is approaching an area where everyone is an enemy, she blinks her eyes and nervously twists her head.

An incoming wave takes her feet off the sand, lifts her up, then dumps her in the sea again. She comes back through the surf to the shore, shell shining with seawater, flippers making their bird-wing motion.

She lifts her head carefully looking at the place where she herself was probably born and where it is believed she returns year after year to lay her eggs. A great and mystifying feat of navigation has brought her across hundreds of miles of ocean to a pinpoint on a strange and dangerous beach.

So remarkable is this achievement that scientists have tried to check out turtle compass-sense orientation, celestial navigation, sense of smell, and homing instincts, with smell seemingly the most logical means of the turtle's locating its home ground. In trying to track down this turtle talent, researchers have attached radios, floats, and balloons to traveling turtles. Thus far there are no conclusive answers to how the sea turtle finds this speck of land to which it returns. It has been proved that loggerheads are skillful mid-ocean navigators and are not indecisive about direction if placed far out at sea. But the scientists are still baffled about the hows and whens and are hoping to turn to space for the answer, suggesting that a turtle-tracking satellite may solve this ancient mystery of the turtle's navigation across the trackless sea.

Now, out of that sea, the immense journey behind her, this turtle begins her odyssey's final, most sensitive, and vital stage. Ponderously she lumbers across the trickling water of the beach, sinking into the sand, her flippers making useless motions now.

Out of water she is a cripple. She can barely move, but she must do what she is doing. Unless she does, her species will vanish from the earth.

She starts across the sand as if it were glue, each step sticky, captive, and tortured—her body straining forward, her head straight out, her back flippers dragging in the sand, her nervousness increasing. But her determination to complete her perilous task overrides all else.

She is being watched by friends—and enemies.

Hesitantly she turns again toward the sea, the surf licking in erasing the betraying drag marks. Front flippers braced against the sand ready to propel her land-clumsy body back into her watery element, she poises, seeming to yearn to return to the moonlit sea.

That mysterious maternal instinct that forces her to shore proves stronger than her fear of leaving the safety of the sea. She slowly turns from the water's edge, moving across the beach. Now she pokes her nose and chin deeply into the sand, holds it there, then moves ahead, pushing a furrow in the sand. Is she smelling this sand, trying to identify it as her home beach? Suddenly she stops, sand dropping from nostrils and mouth, lifting her great head, standing as if chipped from stone, watching and listening for danger.

Although she has an eardrum and middle ear membrane that connects with an inner ear through a long, slim bone, it is believed that she doesn't hear well. Her tactile sense is keen, and she feels vibrations which may be her hearing aid. Her eyes are large, but she is not particularly sharp-sighted. It is thought that she has glands near the eyes which remove excess salt from the seawater and ensure proper body chemistry. It is also believed that these salt glands at work are responsible for the tears often seen in the eyes of sea turtles when they come to land to lay their eggs. Some scientists reason that the tears protect a turtle's eyes from sand when she digs the nest, also that when turtles are on land their eyes must be kept moist to prevent their vision from being impaired.

Nose high, she uses her most acute sense, smell, to detect danger. Unfortunately, the night wind is drifting from the sea, not bringing scent from the land to her. She looks for a long time now at the bare expanse of sand ahead of her. Very particular about where she will dig a nest, she is judging distance and direction before making her ponderous move. Now she starts forward, dragging her 300 pounds across the sand.

Moving in her difficult landlocked slow motion, comparable to that of a man trying to walk in hip-deep snow, she finally reaches a point beyond the high-tide line, where she can deposit her eggs without danger of the sea's surging in to destroy them. Scientists have not yet determined how sea turtles decide where to lay their eggs safely but in test after test have discovered that the locations are nearly always safe from incoming tides.

Exhausted by her effort in crawling this far, she nevertheless starts to dig a nest hole, first clearing a small area with her front flippers, using them like shovels.

Once she has scraped off a light first layer of sand with her front flippers, she works with her back legs, curling the edge of her flippers to convert them skillfully into effective sand scoopers. This is not a haphazard nest she is excavating. It must have not only a roof heavy enough to protect the eggs, but proper conditions of temperature and humidity. It is bottle-shaped; the ball of the main part is connected to the surface by a narrow neck. It is dug this way to prevent large cave-ins that would cover the nest with too much sand, delaying or preventing the emergence of the hatched young. The nest must also be deep enough to maintain an even temperature, yet keep the eggs moist, but not so deep that the sand covering them will not be warm. How deep? Just as deep as she can stretch her back legs.

Here she has dug the body pit, in which she rests and lays her eggs in the real nest underneath the body pit. Using her hind feet, she skillfully digs an 18-inch-deep, 12-inch-wide hole for the average of 125 eggs in her first-of-season clutch, her eyes tearful the whole time.

As she sticks her tail into the nest hole, her eggs (slightly smaller than golf balls, soft but tough, with a dent which disappears as the shell swells slightly before incubation) drop into the hole, sometimes one, sometimes two at a time.

Resting briefly after laying the eggs, she hauls herself out of the pit, then carefully begins covering it with sand, using her hind flippers, one, then the other. She stops raking in the big scoops of sand to pack it firmly over the eggs. Again this is not a thoughtless, hasty operation. The nest well covered, she suddenly stands erect over it. Then she falls—squarely over the covered nest, her hard, smooth, heavy plastron undershell firmly packing the sand over the nest. She does this a dozen times. Still not

satisfied, she uses all four flippers to scatter sand loosely over the entire area, covering all signs that she has dug a nest in that spot.

For some unknown reason, the danger period for those life-bearing eggs buried in the sand is the first two days. If predators do not get them then they probably will be safe for the thirty-one-to-sixty-five-day period it takes for the eggs to incubate.

Maternal mission accomplished, the loggerhead wheels slowly, eyeing the place where she has hidden her offspring-to-be, then turns again toward the sea. She may not enter it as soon as she should. She may be delayed and frightened, but she will make it. And she will never see the baby turtles that will emerge from the eggs she has left behind. Her part of motherhood is finished.

Towering Australian pines form a dark background beyond the beach. Patiently waiting in the shadows of the trees is an alert animal that may be the deadliest enemy of the loggerhead.

In many areas along Florida's coast there is a raccoon population explosion. As a result, the loggerhead turtles are suffering. For these clever raccoons who adroitly have learned to live with man and survive his highways and high-rises love loggerhead eggs and eat or destroy entire clutches.

Archie Carr, a professor of zoology who has made
an involved study of sea turtles, reported that on the
Cape Sable beaches in the Everglades National Park,
where turtles are protected from all human interference,
out of 199 loggerhead nests, 140 were completely
destroyed by raccoons. In addition to the raccoons,
ghost crabs and wild hogs, both adept at discovering
hidden loggerhead eggs, formed such a destructive
team on an island in Georgia that a hatchery had to
be established to incubate loggerhead eggs or not
an egg would have remained.

Fortunately, on Jupiter Island where this turtle laid her eggs, there are friends (as there are on a few other beaches in Florida, Georgia, South and North Carolina) who patrol, driving away predators. They also clear obstacles so that turtles can return to the sea without difficulty. Working in teams, they thoroughly cover the areas where turtle nesting is likely, skirting the edge of the sea on the constant lookout for turtles in trouble. This group of dedicated young men is called the Turtle Boys of Jupiter Island.

Placing almost 100 loggerhead turtle eggs that they have rescued from a raccoon-raided nest in a box, the Turtle Boys take them to an area that they have already prepared, awaiting just such emergencies. The young men work quickly to get the eggs back into the moist, warm, life-giving sand that hatches them. Although these are reptile eggs with tough, leathery skins, they are handled as carefully as if they were fragile hen's eggs.

In a wire-encircled, carefully watched enclosure, the Turtle Boys, working under a special permit from the Florida Department of Natural Resources to reproduce the loggerhead's sandy nest as closely as possible, renest and re-cover the eggs. They work on twenty-four-hour patrols to protect the eggs.

Careful records of all renestings are kept, not only of the circumstances under which the eggs were saved, but of the exact time of finding them, re-covering them, the weather conditions, data on the predator involved, condition of the raided nest, and the number of eggs thought to be destroyed. From experience, the young men also know approximately when the eggs they have reburied will hatch. When that happens, another task faces them.

Eighteen inches under the sand, the length of time depending on temperature and humidity, anywhere from just over a month to two months, the eggs begin that mysterious miracle of metamorphosing from yolky eggs to living embryos to perfect miniatures of parents, a process explained by many but fully understood by few, a process that for loggerheads has remained unchanged for 150,000,000 years.

Erupting from their sandy nursery like corn from a popper comes a steady stream of squirming, agitated hatchlings. The agitation is an important part of their birth.

Hatching usually is at night, often after a light rainfall. Down in the nest the scramble for life begins. Before, they were merely eggs; now they are little turtles buried alive. Too long underground, they will smother. But nature has designed a plan to get them out. Each turtle is important to the other. Once out of the shell (accomplished with the help of an egg tooth, later discarded), the turtles begin a mass squirming.

Scientists Harold Hirth, Lawrence Ogren, and Archie Carr were able to observe this instinctive teamwork action of newborn turtles by digging up one side of a nest and replacing it with a sheet of glass. The turtles on top began tearing down the ceiling of sand; the turtles on the sides scratched the walls. Those on the bottom packed down the sand as it fell on them. Also, when the turtles on top stopped working, those underneath began a frantic wiggling, forcing those above to react and keep the communal effort going. Soon, with the bottom layer of turtles packing the sand down and physically urging those above to keep at it, the whole ceiling fell, and the bottom rose. As this happened, the activity of the entire little tribe increased, each acting as a spur to drive the entire hatch up out of their nest. Hence, if there are fewer than ten eggs buried in the sand, the hatched turtles cannot survive. They need the squirming of many to hoist them up to freedom and life.

The wisdom of nature decreeing that sea turtles lay at least 100 eggs is again evident when they escape the sand nest and start for the sea. This action is similar to that of a crowd of people pushing one another forward to get to a subway train. The little turtles keep bumping into one another; as one nudges the other in front of it, it scuttles ahead. This reaction is a survival chain pulling them to the sea. Experiments have shown that a single turtle, not having a nest-mate to prod it, stays out of motion on a beach too long. Such inactivity increases danger and the likelihood of an alert predator getting it.

Turtle Boys here assist in the trip from the nest across the sand to the sea. This is the most important and perilous time of the newborn turtles' lives. Life or death for the young turtles is decided in minutes. Determinedly they make the long trip from beyond the high-tide mark where they were nested to the water, using all four flippers to propel them. Most work is done by the front flippers which reach forward, then push backward like a boat being oared. It is strenuous work, but the turtles do it quickly or they are dead. Instinct tells the hatchlings this, and the mass movement is remarkable in its unerring direction toward the sea.

Even the baby loggerheads puzzle the scientists.
They aren't sure how the hatchlings find their way
to the sea. In a test case, turtles just out of their eggs
were flown from a beach on the Caribbean to a strange
one on the Pacific and released from a man-made
nest back in the dunes where the ocean was hidden
from view. Without a wasted motion, the entire hatch
went directly to the sea.

Leaving the soft dune sand, perhaps the turtles are
able to tell the difference in texture of the harder
tidal flats or know they are heading in the right

direction when they see waves breaking white in the moonlight. (They can become disoriented by lights from cars on a nearby highway, go there, and be killed; or other artificial light can guide them away from the sea, where they can become trapped in heavy grass, vegetation, or wiry masses of dry seaweed, where they can dry out and die when the sun rises or be killed by crabs.) These newborn have been observed increasing their speed when they reach the land sloping to the sea. They move around obstacles such as driftwood, never losing their direction, and when they reach wet sand, many make automatic swimming motions with their flippers.

But it isn't easy. That path to the ocean is strewn with difficulties. And there is even greater danger waiting from above for them.

If they luckily survive the egg-snatching raccoon and all the other hazards, the tiny turtles still are not secure, even if they reach the sea. An enemy is waiting aloft, swift, agile, deadly, one of the most graceful and fastest of fliers, the gluttonous gull. In Florida it is usually the sparkling white herring gull that looks poetic to men but means death to many baby turtles.

Gulls, like most creatures, also have a built-in survival system that guides them to food, and they are somehow secretly alerted when loggerhead turtles are born and out of their nests. Suddenly they appear and begin their murderous dive-bombing, picking up the finger-sized baby turtles and gulping them. The little loggerheads are soft, easy to swallow, and completely helpless on land. They are almost as vulnerable in the water. For the first week they are buoyant, since the remains of the unabsorbed egg yolk still attached to their bodies make it almost impossible for them to escape by diving. Thus, they are easily scooped off the surface of the water by gulls and other large seabirds.

The ferocity of the birds' attack can be frightening. Veteran sea explorer Jacques-Yves Cousteau and several of his men on the tropical island of Europa were horrified to watch seabirds slaughter baby sea

turtles by the tens of thousands. On this uninhabited, desolate island, Cousteau estimated that about 250,000 sea turtle eggs had hatched or were in the process of hatching when he and his men arrived. As the turtles hatched, thousands of birds appeared over the island: frigates, crows, gulls, bold birds that actually snatched baby turtles out of the men's hands and attacked the men themselves when they tried to save the turtles. Despite the men trying to help, such was the ferocity of the vast flock of birds that fewer than 1,000 of the tiny turtles survived. The men were shaken by the violence of the slaughter, which went on for several nights. The few turtles that did survive on their own made it because they were born on a dark night and escaped even the sharp eyes of the voracious birds. Said Cousteau, "It may seem that nature's way is a way of madness. Hundreds of thousands of turtles sacrified so a few species of useless and disagreeable birds may survive." But he reflected that man's way is little better.

Sometimes the Turtle Boys drive away the gulls and
other predators and assist the little loggerheads along
the beach to the sea. At other times they use the
artificial hatchery and transport them to the beach.
Each summer the Turtle Boys of Jupiter Island hatch
an average of 30,000 eggs, then put the hatchlings into
a protected salt water pool until some are tagged.
(Weighed and measured every two weeks, on a diet
ranging from fish to bananas, in just six weeks turtles

averaged nearly twice their original length and more
than five times their original weight.) Often the release
to the sea involves as many as 4,000 of the tiny turtles
at one time. Some of them tumble over, but they always
manage to stagger to their feet and follow their fellows;
laggards are gently prodded by the boys so that the
troop can take to the water as an intact unit.

In about eight years these babies will each weigh
200 pounds.

Although swimming free in the sea, the newborn loggerheads still are not safe. Here again, nature helps. Dark on top, light underneath, the baby turtles do have some camouflage protection. Seen from above, they can look like green seawater; from below, they can be blanked out, blending with surface light.

It is not known if they stay together in their nest group once they strike seaward. And it is not known where they go. They vanish for at least a year. When they first enter the water, they swim straight out, ducking under from time to time, swimming strongly, surfacing for air. They dodge the big, powerful incoming breakers by diving under them, it is thought; but always they stroke steadily ahead toward that destination where they disappear from sight.

Do they just drift with the current? Could it be that they are swept up into the Gulf Stream and spun into the middle of the North Atlantic to live there in a place of quiet water called the Sargasso Sea? This is a strange area where the also mysterious eels breed and seek refuge when immature—a place of almost no wind or rain, of a higher water level than the other sections of the sea. There millions of tons of gulfweed, or Sargasso weed, grow, plants that float and contain marine life that turtles could eat.

This strange sea turtle, this enigmatic ocean reptile, piles mystery on top of mystery. That is a strong part of its fascination.

The fact, however, that the female adults must come ashore to lay their eggs may turn out to be a firm basis on which scientists can stand and peer into the murky world of this devious denizen of the deep and finally solve the many-sided puzzle of the loggerhead.

Two of the Turtle Boys catch such a turtle after she has laid her eggs and almost reached the sanctuary of the sea. One holds her on her side while the other grasps a flipper and attaches a metal tag to it. The tag is marked with the place and date and can be helpful in tracing the migratory movements of the loggerhead if she is caught by biologists in another area. The size of the adult loggerhead is evident as she teeters between the boys. The average adult weight is 300, but loggerheads weighing more than 900 pounds have been found. The eyes are almost the size of a teacup, the bony beak not much smaller than a man's head. The flat, smooth, horny plates of the plastron look like a section of a medieval knight's armor. It is so flat, and with her great weight behind it, it is clear that there could be no better instrument for stamping sand over the nest. Nature gives each creature the necessary physical attributes to help ensure its survival.

Flat on her back, she is completely helpless. This is the way market hunters transport these great reptiles on shipboard, easily as if they were bales of hay. Seeing this enormous creature on its back, harmless and vulnerable, clearly shows the great danger that has faced these turtles for thousands of years. Mammals other than man quickly learned to flip them over and kill and eat them at their leisure. Lions, tigers, bears, even feral dogs have been observed tipping sea turtles on their backs.

Here this loggerhead is on her back in the interest of science. She is being carefully measured, the date and her weight recorded so that if she is ever recaptured and identified by her tag, her rate of growth can be studied, and thus another blank space on the chart of this puzzling turtle filled in.

Helped off her back, she quickly regains equilibrium, balancing on one flipper gracefully as a ballet dancer. As she goes back to normal posture, the other winglike flipper comes down so that she regains her stance on the sand without landing too heavily.

Her benefactors behind her, she is almost ready to depart the land that locks her in, the land that makes her lose balance and power of movement. Even though she is just touching the water, the magic metamorphosis is beginning. No longer does she look helpless and lost. Now, so close to the sea, the turtle becomes again a perfect part of its environment.

Sea turtles are patient, peaceful creatures. They do not attack man, nor do they harm his land or his environment. In fact, with their annual visits to shore they enrich man's life by bringing alive in their own changeless shell the reminders of a time when man did not exist, a time to ponder. They waddle to shore out of an age of wonder, out of the mists of eternity, making us realize how insignificant we really are, brash newcomers to the world. As such, we should learn from the loggerhead—not by eating its eggs and flesh or invading its nurseries, but by studying the reasons for its fantastic survival despite all odds. Such study might contribute to our own survival.

Measured, tagged, exhausted from her ordeal, this ancient reptile deserves admiration and respect. She has survived millions of years of evolutionary hazards that completely wiped out many species: monsters the size of houses that gobbled everything in their paths; drought that killed or changed many marine creatures; vast ice sheets that swept everything before them.

Soon this turtle we have been watching will vanish again into the depths of the great Atlantic. But as she stops for a while, the surf breaking beyond, the vastness of her world beckoning, our loggerhead seems to wait to be recharged, revitalized by the sea itself. She is part of that sea, its creature stuck with its barnacles (shellfish living on her shell), its marine grass on her back sprouting from patches of slick algae. Her old armor cracked and holed in places, her neck wrinkled, as she rests at the edge of the sea, it is not difficult to believe that she is from a dark, ageless past, so ancient that it boggles the mind to think of the countless centuries she and her kind have paused by the ocean looking exactly like this.

Her age is not known. How many times she has returned to this beach from that far place that only loggerheads know how to reach is also not known. This turtle may be fifteen years old, or fifty. Atlantic loggerheads usually do not mate until they mature at about five, so she is at least that old. No one is certain

how long sea turtles live. A loggerhead reached the age of thirty in captivity. But it is believed that in the wild they can live five times that long. No one, however, has yet been able to keep accurate longevity records. The loggerhead remains as mysterious as the sea itself.

One fact is certain: As long as she has life, the female loggerhead will travel miles across trackless ocean to return to the beach where she was born— to lay her eggs in the sand. By this old immutable law of reproduction despite all hazards, the loggerhead struggles against this new age (of machine monsters, chemical killers, and greedy men) that is the most dangerous of all. Compared to the destructive power of the bulldozer, the dinosaur was a dwarf; beach umbrellas mushrooming in glowing colors on a loggerhead's beach are deadlier than a drought.

For a while yet this fascinating species of turtle is being kept alive by nature's own logistics, the logic being that even if only one loggerhead out of those eggs saved from the raccoon makes it to maturity, there eventually will be more to complete the cycle of life. The Turtle Boys of Jupiter Island greatly multiplied those loggerhead mathematics of survival. Now to save this turtle that we know so little about we must multiply boys and men such as these.

It would be sad for the loggerhead to lose such
a long, hard race.

Make Haste Slowly

This famed motto Festina lente,
the seal of Pope Gregory XIII, was created
and designed, it is said, after the Pope had
observed a giant turtle in motion on land
and reflected on how long the turtle had
survived when so many other larger,
swifter, fiercer, and seemingly more adaptable
creatures had vanished from the earth.